AENGUS' BIKE

SONJA MARTIN
AND
LAURA MCMASTER

Aengus' Bike
Copyright © 2021 by Sonja Martin and Laura McMaster

All rights reserved. No part of this publication may be reproduced, distributed, or transmitted in any form or by any means, including photocopying, recording, or other electronic or mechanical methods, without the prior written permission of the author, except in the case of brief quotations embodied in critical reviews and certain other non-commercial uses permitted by copyright law.

Tellwell Talent
www.tellwell.ca

ISBN
978-0-2288-4475-4 (Paperback)

To all little learners and their families.

Oma, thank you for the seeds.

Aengus loves playing with his superheroes and he can build the highest towers with his blocks. Aengus can name all the dogs at Oma's farm and loves to help her with chores. But, Aengus cannot ride a two-wheeler. Aengus said to his mom "I'm ready for a big kid bike!"

One day, Aengus' mom came home with a shiny, new two-wheeler. Aengus could not believe his eyes. Aengus looks at his bike and examines every inch! It has big black tires, the pedals are yellow, the frame is blue and his seat is red. It is the best bike!

Aengus climbs onto his bike and starts to pedal. He bikes all the way to the fence and then all the way to the chicken coop. It is the best bike!

But, then Aengus notices something; his bike has tiny little wheels on either side of its back tire. He did not notice them before. "Momma, what are those tiny wheels?". His mom says "those are training wheels; they will help you to balance and learn how to ride the two-wheeler". Aengus sits and thinks a little about what his mom just told him.

At dinner, Aengus says "momma, I don't need training wheels, I'm ready for just a two- wheeler". Aengus' mom thinks for a moment and says "well, if you would like to try, we can take the training wheels off tomorrow." Aengus is so happy!

The next day, Aengus' mom takes off the training wheels. Aengus climbs onto his bike, starts to pedal and falls over. Aengus gets up, picks up his bike and bravely tries again... he climbs on his bike, he starts to pedal and he falls over, again.

Aengus starts to cry. Aengus' mom comes to him and says "it was a good try; we can put the training wheels on again if you would like?". Aengus thinks for a moment. "No thank you, I want to keep trying. I want to ride a two-wheeler."

The next day, Aengus gets up super early and goes straight outside to his bike. He practices and practices and practices. And before he knows it, without the training wheels, Aengus is riding his two-wheeler. He rides all the way to the fence and then all the way to the chicken coop. "Momma, momma, come see! I am doing it! I'm riding my two-wheeler". Aengus' mom comes running outside "This is amazing!! I'm so proud of you! Guess what? I just got off the phone with your dad, he says he is coming for a visit this weekend!"

Aengus smiles and says "I can't wait to show dad how I can ride my two-wheeler with no training wheels."

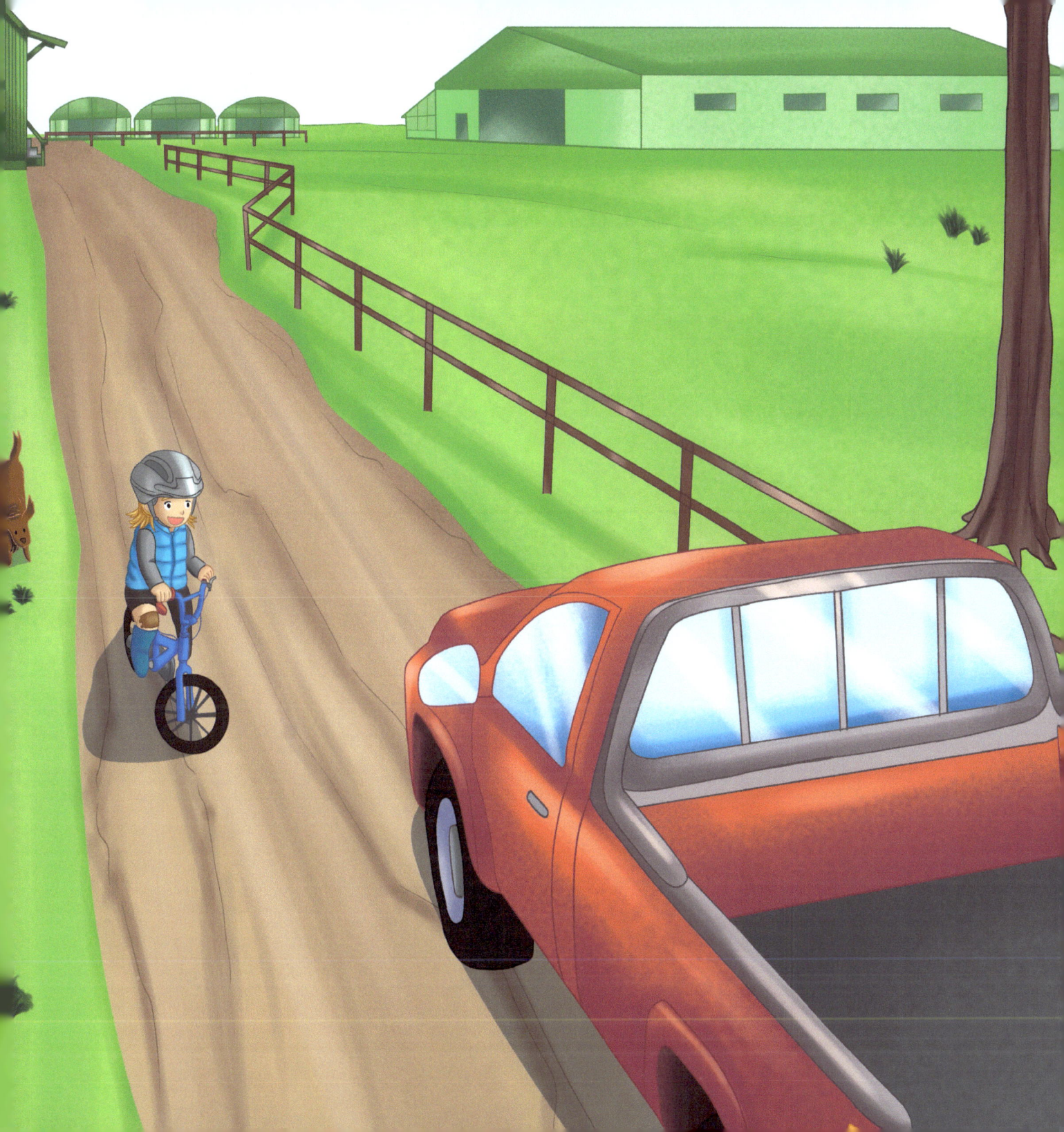

www.ingramcontent.com/pod-product-compliance
Lightning Source LLC
LaVergne TN
LVHW071654060526
838200LV00029B/462